S0-EGI-315

MOVING UPSTREAM

MOVING UPSTREAM

by Mary Barnes

AT BAY
press

WINNIPEG

Moving Upstream

Copyright © 2023 Mary Barnes

Design and layout by Matthew Stevens and M. C. Joudrey
Cover artwork by M. C. Joudrey

Published by At Bay Press May 2023.

All rights reserved. The use of any part of this publication, reproduced, transmitted in any form or by any means electronic, mechanical, photocopying, recording or otherwise, or stored in a retrieval system without prior written consent of the publisher or in the case of photocopying or other reprographic copying, license from the Canadian Copyright Licensing Agency-is an infringement of the copyright law.

No portion of this work may be reproduced without express written permission from At Bay Press.

Library and Archives Canada cataloguing in publication is available upon request.

ISBN 978-1-988168-98-2

Printed and bound in Canada.

This book is printed on acid free paper that is 100% recycled ancient forest friendly (100% post-consumer recycled).

First Edition

10 9 8 7 6 5 4 3 2 1

atbaypress.com

"We all of us are energy...
we all of us are dream and story
and in the end we return to it
to energy, to spirit, to the great
ongoing tale of our becoming"
—Richard Wagamese

Foreword

Voices can come from fragments of conversations; in dreams, in the thunderclaps heard on a sunny day with no sign of a storm, in the silent wind moving the long, summer grasses. They can come as images from a loved one, in the song of a redbird, in the scent of sweetgrass. Coming from the spirits of ancestors, words are meant to be spoken. Written.

As a maker of things, a writer and poet, I want you to imagine the poems taking you from a comfortable place to somewhere new; that you are moving upstream, past sunken logs, stones, and bears searching for sustenance.

As you read, may the words created here carry you, and bring light to your heart.

Contents

You 1

The Way...3

Sometimes 4

Goodness..5

Substance 6

Summer Holidays 7

Shape Shifter...8

Prize..10

Little Spirits...11

Up on the Chena..12

The Heart Way...13

Shape...14

Crow Also Knows...15

Ssh 16

Blessing...17

China Plate...18

Of What Once Was 19

Mal du Pays 21

Snapshot 22

One Summer Day 24

Companions 25

Recess 27

When I Was Yesterday 28

Big Blue..29

In the Silence of Noon.....................................31

The Star...33

Wind and Rain...35

Autumn...36

Old Doon...37

John F. Kennedy..38

Housebound 39
Purple Shoes 40
The Herald 41
She 42
Communion 43
Spring Cleaning 44
Endangered Species 45
Moving Upstream 47
Exchange 48
Walking the Heart 49
On the Last Evening 50
Waiting for the Heart 52
Glowing 53
Apple Slices 54
Before Winter Sets 55
Home 56
Omega Song 57
Heart's Pleasure 58
How Wide the Night 59
Let the Fire of Youth 60
Love Observed 61
Spirit Born 62
The Last Snow 64
Resistance 65
In a Blue Wood 66
Who is She? 67
The Flame Itself: a mystery 68
Point 69
Trapper 70
I Want to Say 71
Dreaming of Flight 72
Gouache 74

When the Sound Comes Round 75

Call Me Love 76

New Order 77

Substitute 79

Temperament 80

When I Walk 81

The Fledgling 82

Longing 83

One More Time 84

I Didn't See 85

Trees 86

We Are Here 88

That Good Place 89

We Will Not Die 91

This Poem Is 93

Grandfather Stone 96

Anniversary 98

Swing 100

The Messenger 102

Summer Visit 103

Blueberries 104

The Memory Keeper 106

The Artist 109

Birthday Present 110

The Watch 111

Nothing Happens 113

Swimmer 114

Flowers 115

Steps 117

Light and Shadow 118

You

In the time of the Sap Boiling Moon
light playing on the wall,
you pushed your foot against your mother
wanting out.
She shook your father
who stumbled awake.
Drove for the midwife.
Wide of girth with laughing eyes, she called to you
                    caught you in her arms.

In the two-room cabin called home
                         cramped for space
you lay
between your father and your mother
nestled in the place
they used to meet
under a moon white as bone
that watched
              their loving.

You mewed
under the new moon
arms and legs stretched toward
that circle of light
your grasp for words
yet inarticulate.
                    Still,
your fingers made eloquent gestures and
delighted them with their own language.

Mary Barnes

The Way

Wauwaushkeshi, she says
and I wonder why my mother does not
simply say, *deer.*

I wait for the story:
how the partridge will thrum
burst from the brush,
how the four-legged one
will flee the moss-covered forest.

I imagine how he will shatter
the river's icy crust
where his brown coat will soon grieve red.

No, she says as if reading my mind.
That is not the way of our elder brother.
He knows when to stop and face the hunter with a fearless eye.
He knows when to offer his body, wait for that shot
so our own will be sated, steady and strong.

It is then I understand the thought behind my mother's words.
I nod my head and say, *Wauwaushkeshi.*

Sometimes

Sometimes when she speaks
her gnarled brown hands roam the air
as if she wants to catch the words
                        passing from her tongue
as if she wants to create them again
in another order,
a language uncluttered with excess,
letters reassembled like the Lego blocks
you had as a child to build boats and spaceships.

Auzhawaeyau-goonidjeeish, she says
and you see thin-veined wings,
a blur of red darting in sunlight
                        hovering
to leave a message
that what you are doing
is at one with Creator.

Then in a breath, it is gone.

Dragonfly, you reply, smiling.

Goodness

You know heart
the beat of your boots
            crunching snow
legs pulling you forward
across the yard into the blue afternoon
March sun
            soft with the promise of spring.
Heart smiles the way you
pour sap into the black kettle
one tin bucket after another
                  fire lit
                  everything ready for boiling.

You think of all the sweetness
you want the world to taste
the headiness of amber liquid
                  on the tongue.

Substance

In her youth
she looked upon the moon and stars,
wondered on the universe
and her place in it.

Wondered as she lay
in her bed on cold-boned nights
why the moon laughed
from its distant place
why the stars only
blinked in their perfection,
whether she should
follow her heart
or listen to what the Old Ones had to say.

When she journeyed out
she did not know where the
road would lead.
Knew only substance in the place
she was born to
the place of trees and refuge
the river of thought
where fish hid in the cool waters —
this kernel of truth –
                        her inheritance.

Summer Holidays

She waits for her son
the boy who is her light,
who knows the English words,
and does numbers in his head
while she tries to accept
the harshness of the white world
knows
as she leans into the June wind
that she stands alone
at the edge of the bush,
            an Indigenous woman,
looking for her place.

Shape Shifter

Last time I talked to your Uncle Fred
he was staring out the barred window in the visitor's lounge.
His days short he wanted to talk:
Long time since I smelled grass, he said. *You know that smell?*
Fresh and sweet.
As he laughed, I saw the boy I once knew.

In these prison walls
        there's nothing.
In here you smell despair
        cold and hard as this cement floor.

Oughtna killed that fella.
Not my fault you say.
Thinking on it now
I'd say I had a choice.

In here I get a cellmate's
hard-hitting hand upon my chest,
steel-toed boots
shoved into my ribs.
In here there is no air
only the sweat of others.

Listen. There's Kaikaik, the hawk.
Hear him on the wind?
Spread your wings and
soar the electric blue

8

swoop and dive through clouds rolling like tumbleweeds
skim sun-bright fields of yellow-eyed daisies.

I think he was a poet, your uncle.

Then he stood
spread his arms
flew away and disappeared.

What I remember most were his last words:
Grass is green, eh?
Even now Sis.
Grass is green.

Prize

You think
as the judge dips the spoon
into the gleaming jar and
tastes the relish
made from September's unripened tomatoes,
from peppers gathered, sliced
and cooked over a slow fire,
a pickle for any connoisseur,
that you will win.

When he smacks his lips
and emits a contented sigh,
your heart beats even faster.

He sees your name on the entry slip,
looks up
at your brown face.

His own face darkens
and frowning
                he makes his choice.

Little Spirits

The July breeze nuzzles her face
flutters off to lift dew
from the frilled fringe of a bearded iris.
An ant, small and black,
climbs her leg
unruffled by her swats,
determined in its search for food.
A ladybug in her spotted coat,
alights on her shoulder   sighs
then whispers:

> *Miigwetch.*

Up on the Chena

there was barely a ripple.
Water held pine and cloud – a world inverted.
Ducks waiting on the sand bar
squawked and pleated their burnt sienna feathers
when he came from the bend
gliding in
        poised
on a six-foot wingspan
his white head
aimed like a spear.
Migizi,
Good Spirit, he is called.

She shivered
under his noble golden eye.
He veered, then melted into the wilderness
And she knew he had gone to speak to Creator.

The Heart Way

With ear bent,
listen to the heart.
Do not rear and writhe
against its energy.

Treat the organ
like an instrument.
Touching the strings
play the tune with gladness
until the end of the song
giving it character and emotion.

Walk neither in bitterness nor regret
for the heart is the muscle
that supports love – the seat of the soul.

Have the heart of an oak and
remember to taste mercy for it gentles wrong
                              as rain blesses the flower

                              as benevolent winds ruffle water.

Shape

Long time ago
Sky-Woman took a scrap of mud
from the bottom of the sea
and fashioned the First People.

Descendant,
I come from a chunk of rock,
a trace of gold,
snippets of bark and wood.
Silver runs through my hair.

I am the flotsam and jetsam
                    leftovers from the
beginning of the world –
                    not complete.

I must dive
into the blue of the ocean
to find a vision
to discover the seed
so that I may fashion
what I want to know
so that I may be like Fox who
                    leaps in the snow.

Crow Also Knows

Wild and lonely is the hill
without the house.

Wild and lonely is the place
where the garden once grew
and the gate stood open
                    to all.

Gone are the wallpapered rooms.
No echo of footfalls in the hall,
                    no more the tree
that shook its branches at Moon
and scraped against the windowsill.

Rain weeps on the windowpane
and I wonder on that wild and lonely place
where once I knew love by the bubbling rill.

Crow also knows
and caws a long
                and desolate call.

Ssh

Look at the trees. The Standing Ones.
See how the snow coats their branches
after the first fall of snow.

Too soon to know if the
winter will be long
nights cold.

Aih, my children.
I want to walk
with the old men and the old women
                      their hands on my shoulders
as they tell me stories
and impart their wisdom.

But now is the time to tell the stories I know.
To honour
the memory of those loved ones.

Ssh.

When the spirits speak
pay attention and listen...

Blessing

In the black night
I dreamt
I knocked at the brown door
of my father's house.

Coming, he called
then stood at the entrance
a smile on his face
yet distant and tired
as I embraced him.

My mother
did not squeeze back at my hug
but placed a purple shawl
she'd been knitting
onto my shoulders
so light you'd have thought
it was a smile.

Walk now with the Old Ones, I heard them say
as I considered the gift, the weave of it
so tight. So strong.

Listen to their words. Learn from the stories.
Then pass them along.
                    It's what we do.

China Plate

They are sifting through
dirt and rubble
in the remnants of houses and barns
abandoned in the Depression.

The boy finds a china plate
cracked and chipped –
Blue Willow –

Thinking it such a discovery
he holds it aloft to his mother
who smiles.
She turns and thinks of the land
before china plates
before iron kettles and wagon wheels.

Wind blew
through fields then
shook tall grasses,
and the People
walked freely
before the veneer of cities and towns –

the heart still bleeds.

Of What Once Was

Except for the ancient rock
standing on the moss-covered grade
that leads to the old vegetable patch
there is no trace of what once was:
$$\qquad\qquad\qquad\text{the house with the sagging door}$$
the brown-stained woodshed
the other outbuildings
$$\qquad\qquad\text{large and small.}$$

There is only the silver-tongued sound
$$\qquad\qquad\qquad\qquad\text{of Wind}$$
as she whistles over grasses
grown long in the years
that have come and gone in our absence.

The idea is that a new highway for the tourists
will run through the land of our childhood,
the hum of cars and rumble of RVs
drowning out the delightful season
that once was solid to us —
$$\qquad\qquad\qquad\text{days full of colour}$$
racing through brambles
in the gold dust days of summer,
building forts in the needle-strewn forest,
skating on frozen ponds,
blue ice sparkling in white winter days.

Moving Upstream

But for the diaphanous mist
that graces memory,
what comes next?

Do we carry acid in our hearts
at the new change in the climate?
What seeming sleight of hand
will it take to bring back that place?

If we sit in a chair and dream,
we could create a triptych
each panel Fern Hill green
and therefore, extend our childhood.

Although stepping into the past
can hence bring danger
tantalizing us with its green essence of longing.

The house is a scrap of memory
like Moon winking her reluctant
farewell at dawn.

Mary Barnes

Mal du Pays

If only we could return
to the shape of love we first knew
the gentle home we now see through mists of time,
the days then lucid where we were content.

What placid days they were:
for we knew the blue-white lace of blue jay,
his song of jubilee in the pine
and hawk, his distinct and piercing whistle on the air,
Father in his work-worn overalls
the swing of his scythe on ripe hay.

Yet when Moon's lantern
bids farewell to the night
I too say goodbye
walking down the hill of memories
on a journey
towards a future
            unmapped and unfamiliar.

Time was ciel-blue and sparkling.

Snapshot

There are four of them
in the black and white snapshot –
three standing on a flat white rock amid
                                    the brambles.

You are on the outside
 one step back
 as if you already know
 your days are short
                    that one spring day you will disappear.

They are grubby
 as children should be, in dirt-grimed clothes.

Grinning. The eldest is solemn.

They are children of the forest,
running in the sunshine
blazing paths of their own,
their voices echoing through oak trees
among raspberry canes
along the moss-edged creek bed.

Each night put to bed in the dusty twilight
by an indomitable grandmother
they think of their absent mother
and wonder: how many summers
do they wait before she returns to the fold?

And will she recognize them
    even though this picture is for her?

One Summer Day

the brothers rode their bicycles side by side
along the old mill road
under a blue tin sky.

Gravel spitting through the spokes
they rode beneath stands of trees
leaves glittering sunshine.

They rode shouting hallelujahs
expanded on thoughts spiritual
talked quietly of hopes and secrets
mile upon mile past brambles and trees
then braked
at the sight of a large black bear.

They did not wait for introductions
nor contemplate a talk over tea
but turned
        breathless
language lost in hearts hammering
and sped towards home.

Companions

You might say
we were companions
each following the other in our daily chores.

Each summer you gave me a perm
and it took all day to set a curl in that rough brown hair
the solution stinking the kitchen
so the stew on the stove,
overwhelmed, almost died.

When the men of the house
worked outdoors with wood and hay,
you kneaded bread on the Formica countertop
as I listened to 78s
while the floor dried.

I heard you sing softly
an aria of your own making
and rapt
I watched the afternoon sun
        glint quietly off the aluminum kettle.

There came a time I had to leave,
take the step that would form my future
you reluctant to let me go and
all the days onward the ghosts of our past
        hovered and haunted our lives.

Moving Upstream

We met again and
snatched up the time remaining
glad the days were there
                    enjoying the walks
along the trails,
the rides in the country,
and on bright fall afternoons
feathery words drifted
across the table accompanied by
                    steaming cups of tea.

Recess

Ran away once in her teens
missing the yellow bus bound for home
not wanting to return to the monotony of her room
                        the same chores,
to the hungry and lonely feeling in her gut
of bottled days to come.

Heart hammering,
she walked down the street
to the town proper
hoping for excitement
like opening a red-ribboned bound package
or seeing the boy with green eyes
who would tell her of things
new and exciting.

Her father found her later
near the A&P.
Slowing down, he said, *what got into you?*
Your mother's worried as all get out.

Somewhere between the river and the rock cut
where the turn off to their place began
she thought she heard hawk shriek
before her heart
                fell away.

When I Was Yesterday

When I was yesterday
the grass green and vibrant beneath my feet
before the fire of age turned yellow
before the silver of winter covered my youth.

There I walked beside glowing trees.
There I made a footprint,
made a mark that illuminated yet I cannot trace
swallowed by twilight's blue shadow.

What preconception had I that I was right?

When the sky above held court
its thunderous judgement a warning
I did not have the wisdom
to change the river of thought
and my heart was aflutter with the newness
of the world.

When I was yesterday
before the fire of age turned yellow...

Big Blue

Acquainted with squirrels,
foxes and deer,
I cannot fathom such a form
as the whale –
Kitchi-maun-maeg –
                in my mother's tongue.

Once, wind whipping my hair,
I rode waves
in a thirty-foot boat
that rose and fell in choppy waters
then slammed down with such force
I felt like Ahab pursuing the Giant White.

Waiting for the vessel to splinter
and send me flying into the ocean's cold depths,
I searched and searched but
try as I might
I failed in my quest for Big Blue
saw only the flip of the tail of the Grey
a shadowy form below the surface of another
and near the shore – sea otters.

Where was this giant with a heart
as large as a small car,
this marvel – a source –
                a fable for storytellers?

Moving Upstream

I heard a fisherman found him

                          somewhere

near the Gulf of St. Lawrence

his heart impaled by a plastic jug

                      breath stopped

no sound but the licking of waves

                          upon the shore.

In the Silence of Noon

A breeze rises
lifting tomato leaves
basking in the sun.
There is little to say about Sunday:
Once the day was holy
meant for prayers and rest
where people lounged on front porches
and watched the sun
drink dew
          from the morning.

Now all is different.

There is
the steady hum of boats
on the river
the whimpering of a dog impatient to be fed
the swish of a car in the street.

There is a woman,
grey-shirted, legs khaki-clad,
engrossed on her cell
cigarette dangling from lips
          dry and chapped.

She passes, smiling briefly.

Moving Upstream

I return to my house
enter my garden
reaching out to
bright tiger lilies,
laced buddleia and Monarchs
                        praising nectar.

That night I dream of the woman
faded and alone
her hair the colour of cornsilk.

The Star

My Darling Red,

Every day I listen for the sound of your voice
scan the heavens for your presence.
Now amidst the whorl of stars I see
the exiled hunter and lover, Orion.
Couched nearby stands his loyal and constant companion,
Sirius.
Forgive me
            but where are you, my friend? My companion?
My fixed star?

Why do I feel as abandoned
as *homo naledi* in his dark chamber
or as the old telephone booth
standing lonely on the street corner?
What bounty is there to this labour of love?
What fruit is there in renewal?

I might as well go back in time,
use an abacus than try to
win back your love. How could I even
conceive of such a thought!

It is the season of burden:
Should I study astronomy?
How can I begin to renounce our love?
Did we not sow the seeds of that affection,

watch as the thin seedling greened and flourished?
Did we not dream
of years of good harvest?

The trilliums will bloom any day now
and Orion will be visible only during the day.
What is that pulsar
spinning towards me from the darkness?
The core of our love lessens now.
Perhaps to solidify into carbon
and later become a white dwarf star or a black one.
Will there then be a colourful explosion before our love
collapses into a black hole?

Oh, what did we reap, dear companion?
What did we reap?

Wind and Rain

In dawn's stillness he waits for her.
There is no suggestion of her coming,
no warning blasts
              not even a whisper.
Only he knows of her kind and weightless manner
the path she takes each time she draws near.

This morning she is late.
He has an image
of disaster that leaves him fraught
with anxiety:
Has she wandered and if so – where?
Was there an interaction on the trail
that has caused this delay?

The day before for some unknown reason she
tipped over the flowerpots
scattered the chairs on the patio.
In turn, he filled the skies with darkness
and flooded the walkway.
She left in a huff
miffed by his scolding.

How to save their friendship?
How do they transform this suspension into harmony?

Autumn

A riffle of wind
crests the waves
plays at your hair –
                    a leaf falling gently

while you slumber unaware.

The pale October sun
scoffs at our love
festering like an angry sore –

                    a leaf falling gently
What is the test
to restore
the bright forest of passion
or to foster the feeling left
                    wrap it around us and pretend we are safe?

Look.
        A leaf falling gently

                    between us.

Old Doon

They took Old Doon the morning
the sun was a pale orb in a grey sky.
He kicked and bucked
but he's been ornery since Brownlee left.
We tried to offer kindness.
He bestowed us with a stamp of a hoof,
                    pawed the ground and snorted his discontent.

Most days he spilled his oats
banged against the stall.
It seems he didn't like living anymore.
He had a home. Dry straw on the barn floor.
He didn't have to pull the plough like his pals,
Ned and Queenie –

Why Brownlee left we still don't know.

Now it's too late for Old Doon
to make amends and start anew.

Yes. They took Old Doon away,
a ghost soon to be seen
                    galloping across the new moon.

John F. Kennedy

The day the president died
I was walking into the next class
         student buzz all around me.

When we settled at our desks
the teacher announced the news
and a hush fell over the room
         soft as feathers falling.

I wanted to do something
         Shout. Cry.
           Scream maybe.

Instead, I hung onto myself,
white-knuckled as if I were
driving around a dangerous corner.

I will always think of French as
         a fractured language.

Housebound

There is beauty in ice
the crystal-cubed shape of
water frozen in a blue beard
                         cold as an iceberg
drifting in the North Atlantic
past beluga whales
white as vanilla ice cream
cut like a diamond
as it slides down the dry desert
                         of my throat.

Think of hockey players
shooting the puck into the net
a bottle of beer cooling in the pool of a lake,
the cellar where Father buried
carrots in pails of sand
                         for winter,
the black glare on the bridge
where the car can slide...

Icicle is melting brown from the eave
on this January day
the sun so warm
you want to open the window
                         and let summer in
but it is a false day in winter
and there is still ice
                         beneath the snow.

Purple Shoes

She wears
purple shoes
on this grey morning.

In the yard
missing him
she touches the earth
          stumbles against grief.

The Herald

To all who will listen:
I am of rivers both large and small
I am from forested mountains
shaded valleys, parched deserts

I am the blue heron
                              long-limbed in the morning sun
the lone wolf calling in the deep night
the silvery fish climbing upstream

I am the man who forges creatures
from metal
                    hammer ringing across the skies

I am the woman who weaves intricate patterns
on blank cloth
                    fingers nimble and knowing

I am the child seeking wisdom in the face of a sunflower.

She

The woman at the party asks:
who is your favourite poet?
I slip into silence
embarrassed I have no reply.

She goes on to say hers is
Neruda. Adds Cohen
whom she has a passion for.

Later in my room
I have my answer.

She is my favourite
the one who tells me
Moon is my grandmother.
She is the one
who waits beneath the lamppost
at the end of the street,
on the path of the forest,
she who comes over the water
                              rushing on the tide
to bring me word
that sends my heart   racing.

Communion

Open your eyes, my children.
See her lightness of foot,
her beauty caught
in the sap green stillness.
Taste the silence and
drink chickadee's
contagious joy.

Spring Cleaning

How long do we scrub corners,
search for dirt
or shake rugs,
watching dust fall on the snow,
       empty wardrobes of needless clothing
kept too long on loitering hangers?

Time to shut the closet door
reach for that clean page on the table,
write something new
dig up words
space them one at a time
for all to see —
       seeds in a garden
waiting to be discovered by
the sun and rain.

Watch the birthing of a poem
burst from the earth and
awaken our sleeping hearts.

Endangered Species

First came the ghost travellers
in their big boats
with white sails
claiming the land
                        as theirs
driving flagpoles into the soil.

Then *Sir* John prescribed
                        —filled the land with
residential schools
our children pressed into
boxes of brick and wood
flattened to shadows
into dark closets
                        away from the light.

I was not yet born
when government men in black suits
and polished shoes
told my grandmother
she could not live on the reserve.
She married out, you see. A white man.
And her descendants
                        became refugees.

I am here on this land
among pines and maples
distanced and separated

45

Moving Upstream

by a river
wondering what place I have
waiting to leap
to a rightful home
         and not feel like an endangered species.

Moving Upstream

You gotta move past the shuffle
down dark lanes
where memories lurk hard and cold
                    past houses broken and lonely.

Ain't no time for petrified fossils.
Ain't no time nor sympathy
for slow-moving salmon.

You gotta leap high through
every spectrum
every sweep of white water
climb past rough and blue-limbed trees
into cinnamon days sweet with the taste
of love
shining on cells
of every green leaf.

Don't go worrying about yourself 'cause
there ain't no surrogate that
can take you upriver
nor any syntax that
can surfeit your soul and make you rise.

Stay fresh and courageous.

You gotta go it alone and
                    keep moving
                            upstream.

Exchange

A cabbage moth,
                plain and white
glides through the yard
tilting around the cedar
while two finches,
                gold and sleek
frolic in the lilac.

I never saw such beauty.

Would I alter my days
and join the hum and din of sidewalks in the city?
Or behold the neon lights
of box stores and video huts as paradise?

Beyond the woodshed,
leaving the telephone
                ringing in the house,
I head to the garden
knowing the walk is worth the conversation
                I will have with the roses.

Mary Barnes

Walking the Heart

The moon through the slats
is a bowl of white fire
not a candle bleeding cold light.

The dog down the street
bays from his yard
his song a single note of pleasure
stirring the night sky.

It is 4 a.m.
a fortunate time
for those who dream
when it is time to move mountains
time to swing from stars and
melt all differences.

A time to fill the blank page
write this poem.

A time for walking the heart.

On the Last Evening

the young couple
walk along the twisting streets
every step a diversion.
                    They reveal nothing intimate.

There is no embrace. No kiss
to forgive the angry words spoken
a short while ago.
They do not seek each other's counsel
nor ask nature to calm their fears.
Nature does not exist here
on the worn pavement
nor in the slumped and shabby buildings.

The device they need is a candle though small
 something sparkling,
 perhaps resembling a roseate evening
                    soft and pleasant –
not a dark and draft-filled room
                    with a dripping tap.

The halcyon shore they are seeking
appears too distant now.
They turn and head towards the hotel
wondering on the experience.

A brown dry leaf
skitters ahead on the tarred surface

and they follow

        holding hands.

Waiting for the Heart

can take a lifetime.
Maybe one, two,
                or three generations.

A walk among the flowers
and you realize
that to scald the heart with poison
drains the veins of goodness,
chokes the voice into deceit.

How do we find the centre again,
                the place that is holy?

The step to set the heart beating
begins with the eye
opening to view waves lapping at the shore
whispering under the fall of snow.

The sleeping garden has the answer.

Glowing

I watch the sunbeam
glide from the chair
ride past the dining room window
along the side of the house
to its western bed
the room chilling,
                    shadows lengthening.

I think of the night so cold
frost snapped and popped
against another house then
a shadow against the moonlight shining in
and my mother draping her winter coat
over my blanket,
the fur collar tickling my neck.

I curled further into the sheets
before it was time to wake up
                    move away.
Until it was time to move the mountains
of a cold and distant future.

Apple Slices

cut thin,
      a Gala,
like moons to be chewed.   Savoured.
                         Swallowed.
While outside the window
the January wind blusters a dark and dense
path through winter.

I think I will write
and let you know I am restless,
weary of the gloomy short days and
                longing for the scent of daffodils.

Maybe if we dream hard enough
the moment will come to this darkness,
and maybe we will know
the feel of spring on our skins.
Maybe we'll hear the heartstrings of new life
in the old earth
and taste the sweetness of strawberries
                cupped in our hands.

Perhaps then we will know
who we are.
          Solid and glowing.

Before Winter Sets

Because the fence is gone
there is no boundary to mark
the place where you kept your garden
where you tried to keep
the chipmunks out
but they found the fruit too tantalizing,
where you found the courage to create
a garden in the wilderness
leaving the pines and birches amazed at your daring.

Without a guide you broke through
 the ferns and stones
 tilling the earth
and settled on strawberries, raspberries and vegetables.

Now only Moon
shining on the trees,
on the crisp new-fallen snow
knows what you performed
                    to make this place holy.

Home

On a morning full of damp and mist I walked the land
until I came at last to the brow of a hill I knew and here
I paused. In the hollow before me stood a house painted
white full of windows and doors. I went down through
the tall, wet grasses. The only one aware of my presence
was the white terrier who watched me with wide black
eyes and then he began to run towards me barking all
the way. If anyone was in the house, they paid no heed
and it gave me the opportunity to mount the steps and
enter through the glassed-in veranda, the dog follow-
ing me, jumping at my legs, sniffing my boots. I walked
down the dark passage into the room that was the
kitchen. No one was about and I helped myself to bread
from a tin on the counter.

In the cool morning
the heart is a country of
gentle white blossoms.

Omega Song

We take this occasion to step through summer along
the forest trail, learning that trees are not only our
companions but our guardians and support. They do
not fumble but lift us up so that once blind we can see
the sky shining blue through the branches. They do not
query or conspire but tell us with authority that we are
their relations, that we are safe-worthy. That we are not
things, nor colours to be denigrated but instead to be
celebrated. They extract from us that we are bodies to
be recognized and accepted unto the whole.

The trees in these woods
are more than summer's bright song
singing, *Hallelujah*.

Heart's Pleasure

Peel a peach.
Let the juices drizzle
between your fingers and
                    down your chin.
Skip down the smooth steps to the yard
onto the grass
lush and wet after a week of rain.
Inhale the scent of roses – Morden Blush.
Watch a fat bumblebee
glide into the deep funnel of a foxglove.

Wait breathlessly for Creator's touch
                    on your shoulder.

How Wide the Night

The moon
              a large petal
pinned to the cold black sky
disappears now and again
behind papery-thin clouds.

And down the way
the train whistle blows
honest and long.

I sit by the stove
picking at crumbs in my lap
from this evening's birthday bash
wondering why the new owners
cut the maple
              back home.

Looking for a solution
that isn't there
longing to sit under its branches
and touch the rough bark
              of childhood.

Let the Fire of Youth

Let children shut the door and fall into deep sleep.
Let them wander through bold dreams by running brooks,
through a dark wood, down strange lanes and not weep.
Let them have no need to beg, borrow or consort with crooks.

Let them not bed down on bricks or starve,
nor be mown by careless shells.
Allow them the pleasure of birches, let them carve
stories from clouds, bestow them with learning's bell.

Let them walk through to the seven stages
with the notion of love – not feigned, fallow or lorn
that can touch hearts, or leap from pages.
Let the fire of youth gather and be born.

Let the mass of goodwill spring to light
and reach far into the western night.

Love Observed

It is a grey and rain-soaked Ontario morning
and words escape me. Nevertheless, they circle and twist
in my mind: What is the use of what we read in books?
Is it cruelty that we turn trees into pulp and make fodder
for fools like me who dither over little black marks on
empty pages? What the spirit craves is sanity:

                              will that make us whole?

Yet there is poetry. My hand on the windowsill,
I watch the trees shake with laughter at my uncertainties
their leaves turning together
in song.

Spider aloft and invisible to the eye
has faith and trusts Wind to help him
                              celebrate life
as he spins his luminescent thread
by gliding from tree to roof to lilac and builds
his web of lace
intricate as a Battenberg or Valenciennes –

                              were I ever so brave.

There is a sudden stillness
 a moment of peace
then a tug from Wind again
that sends the web dancing
as if to say,
                    Well done.

Spirit Born

It was in the time of the Sucker Moon when sucker
goes to the Spirit World to receive cleaning skills then
returns to earth to purify a path for the Spirits.

***

There was no sound where I was. The air was cold. I
was on a journey, an important one but I did not know
where I was going nor why.

A light shone in the sky and I could not see beyond
the brightness. Inside the light hovered a white bird
with wings so immense that it blocked my view of what
lay ahead. Then the bird raised its wings and the way
cleared.

Below in the twilight stood a small cabin, rough-hewn,
with smoke rising from the chimney.

Inside, as if the roof were removed, lay two small rooms,
a kitchen and a bedroom. I drifted towards the bedroom
where the feeble light from a coal oil lamp glowed,
where warmth rose to meet me, where the sharp odour
of a wet diaper spread through the air. As I drew near,
I heard the deep rumble of a man's voice, the soft reply
from a woman.

In one part of the room stood a crib. As I descended,
I saw an infant. A girl. When she saw me, she reached
over and grasped the railing. We recognized each other.
It was then we smiled and she became me and I became
her.

The Last Snow

Under a sky of cement grey
winter lingers
               snow swirling
crusting the lawn in white lace,
the green-tipped buds of the lilac.

You'd almost believe it was
January approaching instead of April.

Look at the cedar branches
caught in a glass of ice
                   undrinkable
       to say the least –
Wind howling
and I want to
              close my ears to her mournful song
praying this fall is the last snow
that green will be what becomes.

Their heads capped in white
the budding daffodils
stand serene, determined to grow.

Resistance

This then, Ash.
Steadfast, rooted in clay and sand,
                                        you wait
while the emerald green borer
nibbles and chews,
leaving trails of destruction embedded in your skin.

One day you may be hewn.
Oh, the ache of not knowing when.

To forget
you stretch scarred and smoke-grey limbs
to the moon's craggy edge
remember sunlit days
when leaves like petals,
oceans of them,
oar-shaped seeds too, a promise of birth,
                                        fell.

Dare lips repeat
this antithesis of Nature
once
whole, replenishing, eternal?

Ears. Eyes. Hearts.
Where are you?
Oh, Yggdrasill,
                Stand tall. Stand tall. Stand tall.

In a Blue Wood

Beyond the ribbon of highway,
beyond the flickering neon lights
the rush of humanity
the lost
        can gather.

It is a wood full of snow
full of mystery
yet intimate and knowing.

There Wind lies still.
There you can pause
dream a journey
unknowing of the road,
unknowing of the footprint
            you will make.
There the western light
will be your guide
and will be faithful
to the vision
        in your heart.

Who is She?

but a woman of soft knees
contemplating love
a woman of the heart
seeking light
like the moon
pinned against
a sky of hope

a woman who says
I am woman
a deep well
drink of me and
rejoice.

The Flame Itself: a mystery

How far to the riverside,
called the miss over the lashing rain.
Less than a mile, I said.
Now why not stop awhile and rest
and have a cup of tea?

Then I noticed the scarred green box
she held underneath her arm
When I inquired she drew it near.

'Tis the flame itself, she cried
and turned towards the village square

'Tis the flame itself, dear soul,
then ran into the rising fog.

Point

is a
rocket to the moon
spearheading
man's search for himself,

is the
author imagining
words for
a story or
the next poem,
racing against time
to discover
illumination.

Trapper

Your father always was good at trapping.
Once with hides on his back
he walked from the bush.
Money in his pocket
he hungered for a bath and
dreamt of a swishing skirt. Mine. Heh!
In town tongues wagged,
voices called across the floor
and spoke of towers that fell,
the slaughter of women in far off countries,
of the boy down the street
who butchered his mother.
Your father downed his coffee,
jingled change on the counter, his face
twisted in distaste. Left.

At the edge of the pavement he stopped and
studied the bush
thought this: the world of the
steel trap and the pain in the beaver's eye,
these things,
were more kind than all of civilization.

I Want to Say

I promised your uncles when
the snow hung like blankets on the trees and paths
I would walk with them.

It's been a long time
since I left the flood plain of my youth
and sought the city lights
since I roared into the intimate world of *things*.
I have made many sojourns, and
along the way here's what I have learned.

Listen and remember, my sons. My daughter.
When you walk into a circle
you will know the truth. There are no corners for lies.

Aih!
Do you see the two wolves ahead?
How they pad closer and closer?
They are my brothers.
I must go with them
into whirling white and step into
the place of quiet waters
where the deep voices of our ancestors
will welcome us
to the fire of a new beginning.
Do not weep, my children.
The journey I make is one worthy of this old warrior woman.

Dreaming of Flight

I feel them breathing on my cheek.
They are great horses dreaming of flight.
They crowd against me. Are outsize.
Smell of sweetgrass. Smell of hay.
'Invisible Presences Fill the Air'/P.K. Page

They trot through dreams I have,
these spirit horses. They govern
my soul, my heart lifting
at each thunderous hoof.
Muscles rippling, nostrils flaring,
they prance before me. Then compliant, almost meek,
they wait; wait for what I cannot see.
With generous snorts, a toss of heads, the swish
of tails, they step forward and seek:
I feel them breathing on my cheek.

One, white as snow, nudges my shoulder.
I turn and breathe into his nostrils.
Run my hand along his smooth neck.
Catching his mane, I mount and
ride on gold-dust wings.
Joined by others we are swift as light,
crossing a prairie of plum and brown,
transparent as the wind
over grasslands.
Galloping with long strides of might,
They are great horses dreaming of flight.

We race by paths unseen into night's blue darkness.
Stars blink on, cold and crisp as ice.
Brightening the way to galaxies not yet formed.
We go on and on, climb the heavens
far from the brown and studied earth.
As we top ancient moon's rise
I see what we have come for:
Not the wealth of nations
Not fame or a grand prize–
They crowd against me. Are outsize.

It is the journey of the heart we seek:

Its gentle nature for love, it's deep and abiding passion,
its forgiveness at the darkest hour
of our souls.
I bend and whisper
my thanks for this revelation. This say.
And carried on night's wind, my message
passes from the lead horse to the others.
Then too soon we swirl downward to day
To smell of sweetgrass. Smell of hay.

Gouache

It is morning,
a mix of grey cloud and weak sun,
a tangle of soft yellows and sage greens –
　　　　　a faded painting from an attic.
Stepping outside,
I walk down the street past
bronze leaves that
　　　　　rustle greetings.

Crows nod,
observe the neighbourhood with beaded eyes
as if they understand my destination.
Squirrels skitter back and forth
along the trail
daring to come near for peanuts they think I have
and above me
a small jet tilts the sky to a patch of blue
while a young woman—one of Monet's flowers
sits bunched on a wooden bench
　　　　　entranced by her cell phone,
her white Labrador
sniffing appreciatively at a pile of leaves.

When the Sun Comes Round

melting winter's battered snow and cheering
the sky blue
we will have Hopkins' days
of May-ness. Cherry and apple blossoms.

Look.
Down past the rows of houses
where the road turns outward
to the bay. The ice piled high
cracks and groans
bound still by the
cold and growling March gales.

There is a longing for warm days
for the shush of waves upon pale sands.
Look across the water to the hills of Collingwood
violet in the sunlight
        lifting the heart

Feel Wind dip
      rise again.

Feel the beat.

Call me Love

when morning skirts the lilac,
when noon's light dances flowers into bloom,
when night embraces the blazing sun home.

I'll be your morning light. You be my
Polaris, my celestial star.
Remember the words that made my skin glow?
Remember the promise we made
that would withstand all upheavals?

Let us look into each other's eyes
behold the joy no marvel can parallel-
no birdsong sweet nor any dawn's stillness.

Through tears of anguish, in moments of fondness,
let us shower ourselves with the knowledge
that love is a blessing-a gift-the kiss
of the sun on the greening leaves of trees.
Let us be each other's light, blazing suns
before that certain night claims our souls.
Do not let me go. Do not let me go.

New Order

Bright berries once grew
in this tangled green.
Willows bent low,
whispered secrets
on the shush of Wind.
Whispers of gifts,
of the care that must be taken.

Surveyors came
pencils sharp, eyes sharper.
Plans grew on reams of paper
scribbled with triangles and squares.
Machines snarled
up the grassy slope and
scooped the soil
shoving aside disorder for order, the men said.
All the while Andeg complained, *Care! Care!*

Ignored
as if he spoke an unknown language.

Tikwaukik
You know that word?
Yes. *In the fall*
hammers fastened nails to floors. Walls. Roofs.
What they made was a shopping mall.
smothering Mother Earth.

Moving Upstream

Then came April on
the soft wings of rain,
moisture trickling
down the mean cracks
of the asphalt forest.
A dandelion
unfolded, stretched, and
pushed its way to the sweet-tempered sun.

Hear its whisper.
Hear its song.

Substitute

She scoops water
from the rain barrel into a battered tin
heats it on the stove

I'm bent over the red and white basin
long hair tipped forward
waiting for the water, now tepid
to sluice over my scalp
waiting for the dollop of Suave shampoo
to be worked through the brown strands
while I dream of places I'd like to see
her strong fingers massaging
                    consolation.

Temperament

It is May
as Wind
blows snow down the bay
coating gardens, lawns and birdbaths
in an eiderdown of white.

Hours later
Mother Nature
chuckles with a warm Sun
over the antics of a boisterous Wind
watching as humans below
censure for her wayward offspring.

How unsettling it is
not to have the seasons follow
in an orderly fashion, say
their voices sharp as nettles.

Oblivious to their groans
the siblings revel in their play
Wind blowing cloud from the sky
Sun melting snow gathered on the daffodils
And their mother
Stirring. Gliding. Urging.

When I Walk

Spirit is beside me
voice soft
so she can hear
Wind whisper in her ear.

She tells me to listen
to the voices out there
in the trees and in the fields
along the road ·
where chicory and Queen Anne's lace grow.

She says to sniff the air
for the rain coming
to listen to *Opitchi* sing
asking the rain
to bless Mother Earth.

She tells me to step around the rocks on the path
because it could be
grandfather or grandmother
and we don't wanna step on them, do we?

And before she disappears
into the heart of the forest
her red skirt swaying
I smile I understand:

To follow the way of the Old Ones
when I walk.

The Fledging

He was hiding
in a corner
of the doorway
cheeping.

When I went
to rescue him
he hopped
down the step
and across the patio
Unto the grass
wings flapping.

He told me as he led me out
into the sunshine
that he was *Opitchi*
and as he left
he sang notes
high and clear
all the way.

Longing

I wanted to invite you
to coffee. Lunch. Tea.
But I sit alone
with my tomato bisque
and a large ginger-molasses cookie.

Looking up, I drink in the
shadow of a man in tatters –
Odysseus – from his long sea voyage?
Or is it Whitman? Or
Ginsberg? Shouldn't he be
at the supermarket?

I wish I could write a poem.

Instead
I hear voices converge
in the kitchen,
the nick of cutlery on china
while cars swish to and fro
outside the café window.

I long to talk to a poet.

One More Time

Snow slides from the roof
leaps onto the cold lawn below
while the cedar shivers
in the cold November air.

In the garden
a robin tilts its head
wonders where summer has gone.

Draped in a cashmere shawl
you linger at the window
and think back
to the days of green
warm with sunlight.

Soon the face of winter will
ice thoughts
slow the beat of the heart
but not before one last journey
to the river
to listen to the water
rush over the rocks
                    laughing.

I Didn't See

My father taught me to see
that going to church
wasn't the only place to worship.

We went to the woods once
where I sat on a stump
while my father, mother and brothers stood nearby.

We looked into the heights
into the light streaming through the boughs.
It fell like a band of golden silk
a blessing onto our heads
warming our faces and hearts.

I didn't see then that
I was sitting in a cathedral.

Trees

Listen carefully
to the birch leaves
as they rustle and whisper encouragement
to walk gently upon the land.

Listen to the poplar
as it tap-taps its warning
to speak kindly of others
to speak to Mother Earth
with reverence.

Listen closely to the maple
to the sap rising
the life force in all things.
It is your life force too
the means with which you grow
you touch each other
you love one another.

Touch the rough and hard roots of the cedar
feel the strength reaching out
to support you
telling you to stand firm on the land.

And when you have listened
to the sounds of our voices
you will walk the roads
known and unknown

and ask all the questions
knowing
     we will carry you.

We Are Here

You tell us to go
back to where we came from.
You call us names
and beat us in obscure parking lots
drown us in icy rivers
leave us on lonely roads.

But we are still here.

We are the possibility
of our people
like the moon
shining in the night sky
over Nottawasaga Bay.

We are always here
our hearts beating
like the drumbeat of Mother Earth.
You talk in your narrow way
that chides us to follow
but the road we know is open.

It is a rough road but full of possibilities
A road where we can breathe
A road where we can meet and embrace one another
A road where we can love.

It is good to remember
we are here.

That Good Place

You know that place
on the hill
where the sun shines
through the maple boughs
and the day begins
smoke-filled with
a threadlike mist
and the bees are humming
their fine tune?
Well, that's a good place.

You 'member
the summers we sat
on the front step –
how many times was that painted –
and talked under the hot sun
listening for Wind to come
and speak to us?
Well, that was a good day.

You think when you leave a place
that you put it away.
It's in the past
has no place in your future
but it's a part of you
rooted in your heart.

Moving Upstream

A place like that is to be cherished.
You don't realize
how precious the river is
or the morning mist
how precious
sweetgrass is
the smell of it
by the roadside
when you walk by –
until you leave
that good place.

Mary Barnes

We Will Not Die

We are on the road
walking towards Sunday
but not towards your church
nor to the houses we live in
you say are empty of love.

You believe you leave us powerless
with the bottle
you gave us Saturday night
with the name Indian
hoping we will forget our place here
on Mother Earth.

But the meadow is not one blade of grass
the forest is not one tree.
We know beauty.
We see the love of Moon and Sun
shining on this sacred ground
where we live.

We know that hearts beat louder
than your voices of condemnation.
We know that bodies
loving each other
hands clasped
spell defiance.

Moving Upstream

You must realize
that in your narrow and tight suit of preaching
because of our passion
we will not die.

This Poem Is

Driving north
wheels humming on the old 69
past dark pines and deep lakes.
Past pink granite sparkling in the sun
standing solid and immutable.
Past the old wooden bridge – gone now –
replaced by steel
to the cut-off on the right.

You look up
expecting to see the house
an anchor to your childhood
but it is gone,
the house demolished for the new highway –
Your childhood slides away.

You go on up the hill
tires crunching gravel
and park to the right
                    brake
and let the motor die.

You think of this sacred place
and the other sacred places you know,
your brothers' split rock
you tried to find once
but gave up knowing it was their place
of solitude and contemplation.

You had a place too
in the dip of land
cushioned with pine needles
beneath the shadow of the trees
where you watched the sky
watched hawk, crow, and blue jay
                          skim overhead
giving you space to grieve
then your mother's anxious voice
calling you home.

You do not reply at first
wanting an answer
to the sudden death
of a brother
the sadness that won't leave
like an unwanted visitor
in your heart.
                    You feel that.

Finally
you wend your way out of
the woods
hop across the creek
calling ahead,
              I'm coming!

Now I'm thinking
of the time
the Old Ones

sent the forest creatures
to guide me.
To listen. To walk the land
to a new beginning.
A becoming.

This becoming
came to live in my heart
and allowed me to grieve
to understand
how we all fit in
how to close the door
gently but firmly on darkness
and open another
to light.

Grandfather Stone

It is late spring
a blustery day
at the beach
when I find a stone –
                    or it finds me.

Smooth and round
small and still in my palm
and I think
through all the hardness
that it's alive
a grandfather spirit
wanting me to listen
to pay attention.

I take him home
and place him with others –
the green and black ones – worry stones I can fit
between my thumb and forefinger
to rub away the disquieting world.

This one is sand-coloured
and as I turn grandfather stone
with vigilant fingers
I see a thin white line
etched there
like a discovered path.

Is this the way I should follow?
                    Seek renewal?

On the other side
is a short band of red.
I think of heart
of my mother
bending to a rose
of Monarchs flitting by
of kindness. Grace.

Miigwetch, Grandfather.

Anniversary

This is about the time
the tiger lilies bloom
their spotted petals
curled towards the sun
near the time our father died –
                    a great tree falling
one brother said
the empty space
full of sadness.
                Bewilderment.

This is about the time
memories birth
at first painful and slow
then each one growing
                    bright and clear
stretching with love
as big as the river
that flows
west into Georgian Bay.

This is about the time
we think
to tell our children
of their grandfather's goodness
how
he placed a seed in the ground
with thick work-worn fingers

willing it to burst open
or
the day he was gentle
when our old red dog, Happy, died
or
when he took us outdoors
on a cool August evening
along about dusk
fireflies blinking, bats swooping
his eyes fixed to the northern sky
filled with green and blue swirls
his form a black shadow
hands splayed on hips

and said,
Look at that!

Swing

Her father
built a swing from
rope slotted to a pristine board.
Looped it over the oak bough. She
sprang forward
rode to places she never imagined:
sailing dirt roads,
soaring over glistening bays
beyond train whistles
to the far side of the wind.

When her journey ended,
she returned home
floated towards him
where he steadied the rope
stilled her wandering heart.

Then she left childhood,
not hearing the brown disappointment in his voice,
not seeing the blue bent of his shoulders
so gorged on rumours of the exotic
                    fed to her by friends and books.

The rope is gone now
rotted to insubstantial strands,
the board grey,
almost one with the earth.
Gone too is her father

on a journey of his own.

Here she is then
glad she's remembered the bough.
She sees her father's wisdom:
that she is the rope
the swing
where dreams begin.

The Messenger

The day she waited
at the hospital
apprehensive of the test ahead
carts clattering by
nurses walking to and fro.
A woman
hunched with age
came into view.
She wore a navy-blue coat and hat and
over her wrist
she carried a handbag like the English queen.

She paused
regarding the younger woman
with sharp pale blue eyes
a slight smile
playing across her worn face.

Good luck, she said before passing
And she wondered
before the old woman disappeared,
What spirit is this?
                    Mom?

Summer Visit

Uncle, auntie, and cousins
arrive while it is dark.
Doors close. Floors creak.
A voice rumbles,
Traffic was light - Good time to travel.

Mother whispers instructions,
Put her there.
        Let him sleep with the boys.
Better grab some shut-eye.

The house settles,
it is quiet once more.
Arms and legs become tangled in bedclothes
in dreams where we run and romp
before the sun
wakes us to a day
green with promise
and bold with play.

Blueberries

We did that
times the summers were high
carrying pails and baskets
no breeze
as we
climbed rocks
stepping over lichen
                looking
sought them
near oaks
the bushes
heavy and succulent with fruit
some years the size of grapes.

We settled to picking
calling out,
                Hello
if separated
in case of bears
juices staining
mouths and fingers.

Weary
almost asleep in the car
we returned home
and later
in the kitchen
bowls of blueberries

on the table
with dashes of sugar and milk
thick slices of bread with butter
                         the best supper
a taste of wilderness
in every spoonful
                when summers were high.

The Memory Keeper

Every summer I came to stay
we'd sit at the table
two cups of tea between us
her lined face quiet and eyes thoughtful.
She'd draw out
photographs – faded, black and white – from
the brown tin
a picture of the old king and queen on the dented lid
and sifting through them
she began
telling me of the people:
Auntie Sue with her kindness
Auntie Julie
who came to the farm from far away,
and Auntie J
who kneaded bones and lived
in the American West.

Next came the men
the grandfather who managed the village store
the one who was chief,
and Uncle Jim who liked horses.

The names passed over me
spilling from her lips
so many ancestors
that walked this good earth.

Mary Barnes

She told me of the big sickness – TB—
of ghost horses
of dogs that barked
in the night
but weren't there
my mind
big with hunger for more.

Young, I didn't know
that this was a teaching
that I was being blessed.

She's gone now, the storyteller
but I remember
those drowsy afternoons
stories riding around me
images tumbling
so many that I could barely
hold onto them.

We'd sit, listener and storyteller
our tea growing dark and cold
until it was time to rise
chairs scraping against the tiled floor
stuffing the brown tin
with the memories
we had stirred
shutting them in
with the dented lid
then gathering the lunch dishes

Moving Upstream

yet to be washed
the afternoon
slipping into a golden hum.

The Artist

When Light
flew through the starry skies
illuminating the dark
past a congregation of cloud
shimmering pink and gold
she paused on the dull slates
of the city's rooftops
before nudging the trees in passing
their boughs stretched
to meet the mackerel sky
then travelling down the street
she slipped past the open window
into the dim and dust-filled room
alighting on the canvas.

Winged. Acute. Expectant.

Ssh.

      Vermeer's painting.

Birthday Present

No money for a gift
nor the necklace she longed for
but he provided her
with awesome tales
festooned shadows on the wall
with broken-nailed fingers
maneuvering her into laughter
so she did not miss the unmuchness
hovering by.

He devised exotic animals and gothic creatures
winging their way to the ceiling
a killer whale or two
then glowing with tea
she retired
unaware the bayonet of poverty
was stayed for another day.

The Watch

The evening is cold
Jack Frost snapping trees
in the woods behind the house
our boots crunching on the snow
as we wait
for our father's return
where he's worked all day
at the mill
cutting logs
      skidding some.

Sometimes, if winds were high
the men worked inside
maybe shoed the horses.

Today was good
the day clear and cold
a time we tobogganed
        on the hill
cheeks glowing
fingers and toes tingling.

In the growing dark
a wolf howls
and we shiver
wonder how far
our father is now
      –he must be cold walking –

Moving Upstream

A shadow moves
on the snow-packed road
        arm swinging
the glint of the lunch pail
intermittent in the moonlight.
We break into a dash
down the shovelled drive
to see who will carry
it the rest of the way home.

Mary Barnes

Nothing Happens

Do you ever wonder
where a black swallowtail butterfly
                    blue-jeweled tail
goes
after you've seen it alight
on a pink coneflower?
You run for the camera
but return to discover
the butterfly gone.

You wait.

The afternoon lengthens
A hummingbird flits by
                    and a bumblebee
hums busily at the bee balm.

Nothing happens.

You feel unfinished
as if you've missed
a suddenness in the universe
like a star
            falling
and no one noticed.

Swimmer

Long limbed
poised
feet
pressed upon the rock

joyous

she p
     l
       u
         n
           ges
down
the dark pool of poetry
words
awakening
her soul.

Flowers

A fine spring day
and you go for a walk
down the drive
along the tree-lined dirt road
towards the mill.
It seems too early for flowers
when you spot them in the gloom
violets beneath the rising ferns – parasols.
Mayflowers
pink-striped
almost hidden
                    shy
too delicate to be picked.

But you do –
this was years before others would say
to leave them be
and enjoy them in passing.

In the kitchen
you find a small Mason jar
filling it with water
set the flowers gently in the jar.

You want to look at nature
on the windowsill –
to capture art
in a bottle.

But they do not last.
You almost hear the sigh
as their heads droop gently
against the rim.

Steps

Buffeted by coin and the giddy lights
she steps away from the Big Smoke
stands calmly under a lowering sky
feet shod in Sorels
                    against the snow and cold.

Once she walked barefoot on June-grass
beneath a drunken moon. Once she was
fearless in the days of youth
but now turning the page
                    scrawled with the marks of time
she seeks pleasure in the days left,
                    fair or otherwise.

What smoke and mirrors we endure
so we can reach wisdom – oh to murder time –
hoping we are not lost.

                    Hoping for a feather.

Light and Shadow

Time goes too quickly
the fog of memory
creeping in
to obscure words and images
and change meaning to a mere
shadow of what it once was.

I soon become a voyager
on a journey to a new land
where I meet dense forests
and deep rivers
unsure of my steps
how to enter the timberland
how to cross the river and
plunge past the rapids to an easy flow.

It's light and shadow.

In one instance I see a bright face
a light in the eyes
in the voice.
In another
the face lies in shadow
and I hear only the voice.

At first
       I am bewildered
by this quality

Mary Barnes

by the howling wilderness
of confusion.
I hear the words again
and they become a lamp
an awareness to direction.

As I find my way
out of the hinterland.
out of the fog of memory
a happiness surges
through my heart
that I can arrive
with hope
that light and shadow
are twins of each other
that I must accept both
on this story
       I am travelling.

Acknowledgements

Writing this book made me realize that I couldn't have done it without the help of a wonderful group of people. A huge thanks to Matt Joudrey (At Bay Press) for taking the leap with me towards publication. Also, to Matt Joudrey and Matt Stevens for the book cover design. The fish is dazzling. To Priyanka Ketkar for her persistence and keen eye, to Danni Deguire for helping me over the periods and commas. A special thanks to my husband, Bob, to Brenda, Tim, and John, our children who are ever supportive.

Notes

1. "Old Doon" was inspired after reading Paul Muldoon's poem, "Why Brownlee Left" from Selected Poems 1968-2014, Farrar, Straus and Giroux, 2016.

2. "John F. Kennedy" was inspired after reading "Rosa Parks" by Sneha Madhavan-Reese in the Best Canadian Poetry, 2016, Tightrope Books, 2016.

3. The haibuns (a combination of prose and haiku created in Japan), "Home" and "Omega Song" were inspired after reading Basho's Journey, translated by David Lundis Bamhill, State University of New York Press, 2005.

4. 'Recess" was inspired after reading "Runaway Dreams" by Richard Wagamese in Runaway Dreams, Ronsdale Press, 2011.

5. I am grateful to P. K. Page's book, Coal and Roses, Porcupine's Quill, 2009, which introduced me to the form, *glosa*, and inspired me to write "Dreaming of Flight".

Ojibwe Glossary

There are many spellings of the following words depending on dialects and pronunciations. I have followed those outlined in the Anishinaubae Thesaurus by Basil H. Johnston, Michigan State University Press, 2007

wauwauskeshi	deer
auzhawaeyau-goonidjeeish	dragonfly
kitchi-maun-maeg	whale
miigwetch	thanks
migizi	bald eagle
kaikaik	hawk
opitchi	robin

MARY BARNES is of Ojibwe descent. She is a graduate of the University of Waterloo and a winner of the Tom York Award for short fiction. She has written book reviews for The Antigonish Review and currently writes for Prairiefire. Her poetry has appeared in literary journals such as the Prairie Journal, Tower Poetry Society, and Voicings. Inspirations for her writing come from the landscape of her youth and everyday encounters. Her first collection of poetry *What Fox Knew* was released in 2019 by At Bay Press and received two award nominations; The League of Canadian Poets Pat Lowther Award and the Manuela Dias Award. Born in Parry Sound, she now lives in Wasaga Beach with her husband Bob and writes, gardens, and talks to the birds.